R.E.Atkins

PALGUE 1·2·3
OF TAE KWON DO HYUNG

PALGUE 1·2·3
OF TAE KWON DO HYUNG

by Kim Pyung Soo

DEDICATION

To Mr. Un Yong Kim, President, Korea Taekwondo Association

OHARA Ⓟ PUBLICATIONS, INCORPORATED

BURBANK, CALIFORNIA

ACKNOWLEDGEMENT

The author is indebted to, and extends sincere thanks for the invaluable assistance rendered by Messrs. K.B. Kim, Yang K. Moon, B. H. Riefchol and Ray Wathen for their editing skills; and John Murray for his photography.

©Ohara Publications, Incorporated 1973
Printed in the United States of America
Library of Congress Catalog Card Number: 73-85437

Eight Printing   1980
ISBN 0-89750-008-3

ABOUT THE AUTHOR

Kim Pyung Soo, a native of Seoul, Korea, attended the Han Kuk University of Foreign Studies where he received a B.A. degree in Russian language and literature. Mr. Kim began studying tae kwon do at an early age under the guidance of Nam Sok Lee, president of the Chang Mu Kwan Association in Seoul. He received his sixth dan from the Korea Tae Kwon Do Association in 1968. In 1970, Chul Park of the Kangdukwon Mudo Association promoted him to seventh dan, establishing Mr. Kim as one of the highest ranked karate instructors in the United States.

During years of intensive practice and teaching, Mr. Kim has taught countless numbers of students, including the Secret Service of the late Korean president, Syngman Rhee, U.S. Army units in Korea, municipal police departments, youth organizations and students at universities in Korea and Texas. From 1965 to 1968, Mr. Kim served as the first Korean news correspondent to BLACK BELT MAGAZINE.

Mr. Kim arrived in the United States in January, 1968 and has maintained a central school in Houston, Texas since September of that year. In September, 1970, he inaugurated a tae kwon do system entitled Cha-Yon Ryu (Natural System). Fluent in the Korean, English, Spanish and Russian languages, Mr. Kim plans to travel throughout the world teaching the spiritual, as well as the physical aspects of tae kwon do.

PREFACE

This is the first book to present tae kwon do as practiced by the Korea Tae Kwon Do Association. Designed primarily for the beginner, the volume covers the first three *Jangs* (sections) of the *Palgue Hyung* (the required form of the first eight grades of tae kwon do instruction).

Tae kwon do has been practiced for centuries as an unarmed defense technique and healthful exercise. Many martial artists have come to learn the Buddhist principle of self-cognizance. Self-cognizance cannot be achieved by the practice of tae kwon do techniques alone, but must be accomplished by a combination of religion, education, self-thought, and other philosophical virtues. The author feels he has found his self-cognizance through persistent training in both physical and spiritual tae kwon do principles.

Many people spend their entire lives searching for such a principle. Consequently, many of the problems in society today are caused by those who, in their early lives, were not given appropriate guidance toward the search for self-cognizance. A person receives his physical body from his parents, but often the spiritual guidance to harmonize that body with the soul is lacking. This is where tae kwon do enters the picture. It strengthens one's body and, if practiced in its truest sense, nurtures the mind as well. The body-plus-mind principle guides one along a favorable path of life.

Tae kwon do—and various martial arts such as judo, karate, kung-fu, and kendo—originated to satisfy the need for self-preservation as man defended himself against wild animals and human enemies. Through the centuries, tae kwon do has developed and broadened into multi-aspectual principles and theories of a physical and spiritual nature, leading to rewards greater than a mere knowledge of self-defense. Regular practice of tae kwon do forms, movements, and techniques has vitalized the author's physical and mental coordination and enhanced his self-confidence and control.

This book is presented with the hope that those who study the art of tae kwon do will not only apply, but share their learning with others, so those who seek such guidance may take their first step along the path to a better way of life.

Kim Soo
Houston, Texas
June 15, 1973

CONTENTS

WHAT IS TAE KWON DO ?

Tae kwon do is the name of a Korean free-fighting, self-defense art that employs the bare hands to repel an enemy. In earlier times, people living simple lives lacked physical strength and agility. To compensate for limitations in their size and strength, the people used tae kwon do as a means of self protection during enemy attacks. Since tae kwon do was developed in this nature, all of its activities are based on defensive tactics. Tae kwon do, as well as being a martial art, is also recognized as a beneficial method of improving health, balance, agility and poise.

A tae kwon do hyung (form) is comprised of approximately two-dozen interrelated stances from which various blocking, striking and kicking techniques are executed against a number of imaginary attacking opponents. These techniques are delivered with the hands, fists and feet toward vital points of an opponent's body. The stances vary according to particular situations throughout the form: back stance, cat stance, horse-riding stance, etc.

Two distinct types of competition are embodied in tae kwon do: free style and prearranged. During free style competition, contestants may use any technique they have acquired in their training for either defensive or offensive purposes. In the prearranged style, both competitors follow a rehearsed sequence of techniques, usually for practice or demonstration. Practitioners must become thoroughly proficient under prearranged conditions before they can adequately compete in free style competition.

Breaking is a method of displaying the speed and power the human body is capable of attaining through tae kwon do training. Breaking is utilized as a demonstration of a practitioner's skill against inanimate objects such as wooden planks, roof tiles, and bricks. Breaking provides an acceptable method of fully applying tae kwon do techniques without inflicting injury upon another person. Thus, tae kwon do is the result of form (hyung), competition (dae-ryun), and breaking (kyukpa).

The white tae kwon do uniform, which symbolizes purity and origin, is neither expensive nor luxurious. Designed to allow freedom of movement, the uniform fits loosely around the body. The student wears a colored belt designating his degree of graded proficiency in the art. In ascending order, the belt grades are white (beginner), blue (sixth to fourth grades of keup), red (third to first keup), and black (the first grade of dan or over).

HISTORICAL BACKGROUND
OF TAE KWON DO

The origin of tae kwon do can be traced to the Koguryo Dynasty, founded in 37 B.C. in the Manchurian province of Hwando. Mural paintings, discovered among the ruins of royal tombs built between A.D. 3 and A.D. 427, reveal scenes of tae kwon do in practice. These tombs, *Muyong-chong* and *Kakchu-chong*, were uncovered by Japanese archeologists in 1935 at Tungku, Chian county, in the Tung-hua province of Manchuria.

The ceiling of the Muyong-chong features a painting depicting two men facing each other in tae kwon do postures while the mural paintings in the Kakchu-chong portray two men wrestling. In reference to the latter painting, Japanese historian Tatashi Saito

The ceiling of the Muyong-chong, a royal tomb of the Koguryo Dynasty, bears this mural depicting two men assuming tae kwon do postures. The tomb was excavated in Manchuria by a group of archeologists in 1935 and is believed to have been erected between 3 A.D. and 427 A.D.

says in his *Study of Culture in Ancient Korea*, "The painting either shows us that the person buried in the tomb practiced tae kwon do while he was alive or it tells us that people practiced it, along with dancing and singing, for the purpose of consoling the soul of the dead." Because the dates of the two tombs parallel the existence of the Koguryo Dynasty, it can be assumed that people under Koguryo rule practiced tae kwon do during that period.

Tae kwon do was also evident during the Silla Dynasty (57 B.C.—A.D. 668). Silla was a kingdom founded in the southeastern part of the land, roughly 20 years before Koguryo in the north. At Kyongju, the ancient capital of Silla, two Buddhist images

At Kyongju in southeast Korea, a stone Buddha sits in meditation guarded by two statues in tae kwon do stances. The figures are located in Sokkuram, a ruin of the Silla Dynasty.

portraying two giants facing each other in tae kwon do stances are inscribed on the Keumkang Giant Tower at Sokkuram in Pulkuk-sa Temple. Silla was famous for its *Hwarang-do*, wandering knights who practiced martial arts. Hwarang-do played an essential part in Silla's struggle to unify the entire country by conquering both Koguryo and Paekche. Scattered evidence contained in the two oldest documents of Korean history, the *Samguk Sagi* and the *Samguk Yusa*, shows that Hwarang-do knights also practiced tae kwon do in their basic training of the body.

During the Koryo Dynasty (A.D. 918-1392), tae kwon do (then called *subak*) was considered more than a health and sports

activity. It was encouraged as a martial art of considerably high value, as the following quotes from the historical record of Koryo illustrate: "King Uijong admired the excellence of Yi Ui-min in subak and promoted him from Taejong (military rank) to Pyolchang. The king appeared at the Sang-chun Pavilion and watched subak contests. The king watched subak contests at Hwa-bi Palace." The records indicate that subak in the Koryo Dynasty was also practiced as an organized sport that could be presented as entertainment.

Subak gained its highest popularity during the reign of King Uijong (A.D. 1147-1170). This period roughly corresponds to the era that includes part of the Chinese *Sung* and *Ming* Dynasties. During this time the Chinese *Kwonbop* form of self-defense became popular after it was developed into two advanced systems, *Neikya* and *Weikya*. The two systems differ primarily in that one serves as a defensive skill while the other employs offensive moves. This fact shows us that tae kwon do is not only of pure Korean origin, but it has also developed independently throughout the long history of Korea.

Subak gained further importance in the Yi Dynasty (A.D. 1392-1910) when a book was published to teach the game as a martial art. Quickly, Subak became as popular among the general public as it had been when monopolized by the military in the Koryo Dynasty. Records also indicate that Subak was once used in competition between two provinces, Chung-chong and Cholla, and the royal government required its employees to know the art. In addition, King Chongjo published "Muye Dobo Tongji," an

Found in the Sambo-chong ruin, this Koguryo era mural depicts a warrior employing a bare hand tae kwon do technique entitled "Muin-Kongsung-do."

illustrated textbook on martial arts which included tae kwon do as one of its major chapters. It is obvious, therefore, that Subak attracted much attention from both the royal court and the general public during the Yi Dynasty.

In the latter half of the Yi Dynasty, however, Subak's popularity declined. The royal court, which once encouraged participation, grew disturbed by strife between feuding political factions and decreed that Subak would be practiced merely as a recreational activity.

Tae kwon do has continued to grow as a martial art in the twentieth century. The art became an affiliate of the Korea Amateur Sports Association in June 1962. The following October, tae kwon do became an official event at the 43rd annual National Athletic Meet. In August 1965, the title Korea Tae Kwon Do Association was adopted.

TARGET AREAS

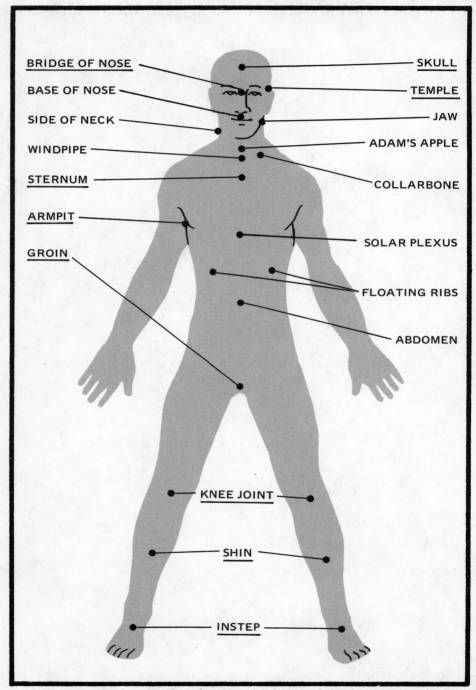

BRIDGE OF NOSE

BASE OF NOSE

SIDE OF NECK

WINDPIPE

STERNUM

ARMPIT

GROIN

SKULL

TEMPLE

JAW

ADAM'S APPLE

COLLARBONE

SOLAR PLEXUS

FLOATING RIBS

ABDOMEN

KNEE JOINT

SHIN

INSTEP

During competition, no attack on the parts printed with underlined letters is permitted.

TARGET AREAS

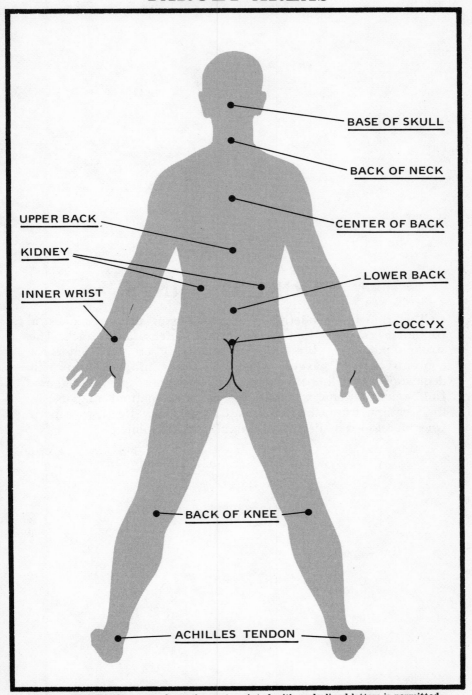

BASE OF SKULL

BACK OF NECK

CENTER OF BACK

UPPER BACK

KIDNEY

LOWER BACK

INNER WRIST

COCCYX

BACK OF KNEE

ACHILLES TENDON

During competition, no attack on the parts printed with underlined letters is permitted.

STRIKING POINTS

The principle underlying all tae kwon do techniques is maximum concentration of power for defense and attack. The striking points on the limbs of the body are the centers of concentration of power. When one trains properly and with dedication, the limbs become true weapons for self-defense. Unlike conventional weapons, the limbs are natural weapons. In their natural form, the limbs can only become effective weapons when developed by dedicated training and discipline.

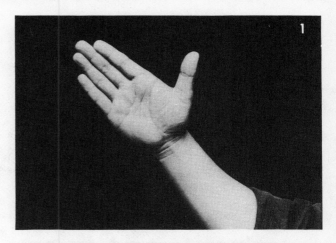

FIST
(Ju-mok)

To clench the fist properly: (1) open your hand, (2) clench four fingers, and (3) press your thumb down against your index and third fingers to complete the proper fist.

FOREFIST
(Ju-mok)

To form a forefist, follow the identical instructions for shaping the fist. Keep your forearm and wrist straight for delivering striking force and avoiding injury to the fist.

SIDE VIEW

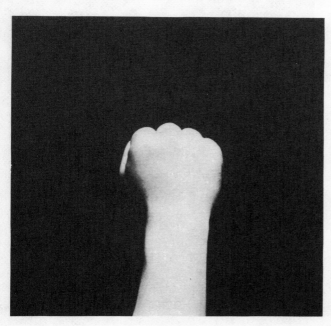

BACK FIST
(Dung Ju-mok)

To form a back fist, follow the identical instructions for shaping the fist. Use the back fist for striking the temple, chin, jaw, ribs, and solar plexus.

BOTTOM OR HAMMER FIST
(Me Ju-mok)

To form a bottom or hammer fist, follow the identical instructions for shaping the fist. Use the hammer fist for striking the head, wrist, elbow joint, ribs, and solar plexus.

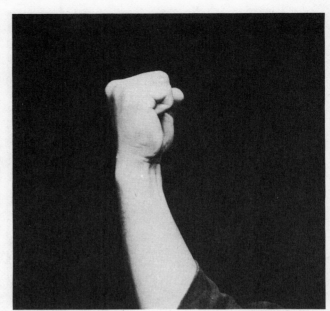

OPEN KNUCKLE FIST
(Pyun Ju-mok)

Bend and press your second and third knuckles hard against the inside of your first knuckle. Bend and press your thumb hard against your index finger. Use the open knuckle fist for striking the temple, below the nose, and points between the ribs and throat.

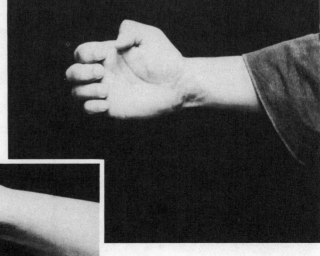

VARIATION

21

CHESTNUT FIST
(Bam Ju-mok)

To form a chestnut fist, follow the identical instructions for shaping the fist, extending the second knuckle of your third finger outward. Use the chestnut fist for striking points just below the nose, between the ribs, and at the temple and throat.

INDEX FINGER
FIST
(Inji Ju-mok)

To form an index finger fist, follow the identical instructions for shaping the fist, extending the second knuckle of the forefinger outward. Apply the index finger fist as an alternative to the chestnut fist if you cannot clench the chestnut fist forcefully. Striking points for the index finger fist are similar to those for the chestnut fist.

SPEAR HAND
(Kwan-su)

To form the spear hand, bend your thumb and extend your fingers as shown. The four fingers of your hand should be held tightly together with your first three fingertips forming a blunt edge. Apply the spear hand for striking the throat, ribs, and solar plexus.

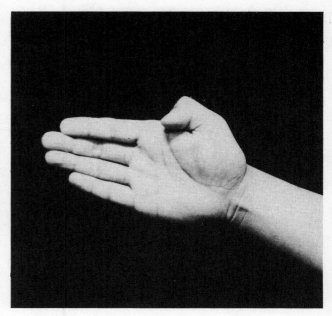

ONE FINGER SPEAR HAND
(Han-son Kwan-su)

To form the one finger spear hand, rigidly extend your forefinger. Apply the forefinger in striking the eyes and solar plexus.

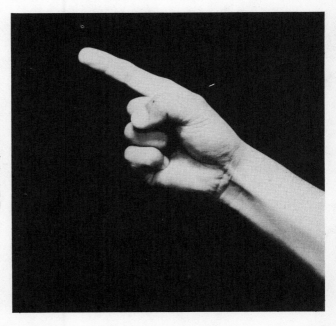

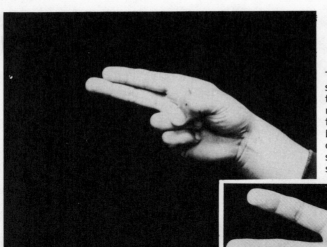

TWO FINGER SPEAR HAND
(Du-son Kwan-su)

To form the two finger spear hand, rigidly extend your fore and middle fingers. The two finger spear hand can be applied in a spread or closed manner for striking the eyes and solar plexus.

VARIATION

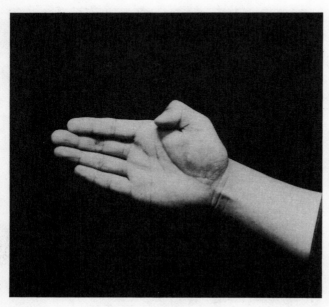

KNIFE HAND
(Jang-kal)

To form the knife hand, extend your fingers, bent at the second knuckles until your hand is tight. Apply the knife hand for striking and blocking the neck, ribs, temple, and solar plexus.

RIDGE HAND
(Oppun Jang-kal)

To form the ridge hand, follow the identical instructions for shaping the knife hand. Apply the ridge hand for striking the neck, ribs, temple, kidney, and solar plexus.

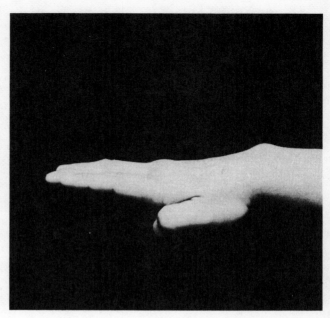

ELBOW
(Pal-kup)

To form the elbow, bend your elbow inward at the joint. Apply the elbow for blocking and striking the chin, jaw, ribs, back, and solar plexus.

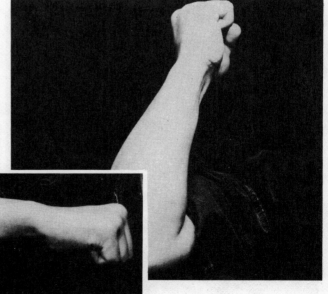

VARIATION

BENT WRIST
(Kom-be-son)

To form the bent wrist, sharply bend the wrist inward with your fingertips locked together. Apply the bent wrist for blocking and striking the chin, jaw, groin, and temple.

PLIERS HAND
(Jip Gae-son)

To form the pliers hand, bend your thumb and forefinger at the knuckles while tightly closing your other three fingers. Apply the pliers hand for striking the Adam's apple.

RAKE HAND
(Gal-qui-son)

To form the rake hand, extend your bent fingers outward, simulating a claw. Apply the rake hand for offensive clawing.

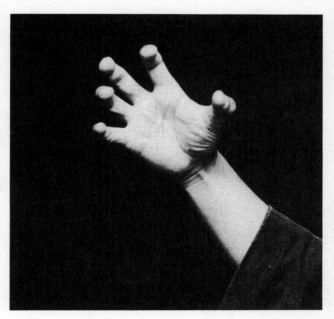

PEACOCK HAND
(Son-kut Cho-ki)

To form the peacock hand, tightly compress your fingertips together. Apply the peacock hand for striking the groin, temple, and eyes.

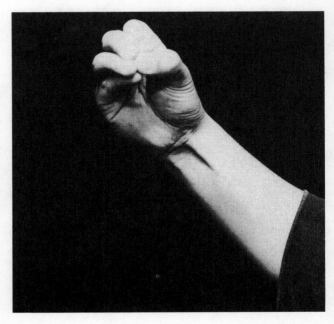

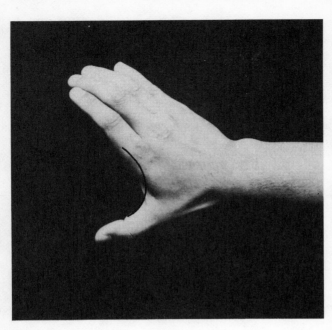

TIGER MOUTH HAND
(Ah-kum-son)

To form the tiger mouth hand, widely separate your thumb from your extended fingers. Apply the tiger mouth hand for striking the Adam's apple (throat area).

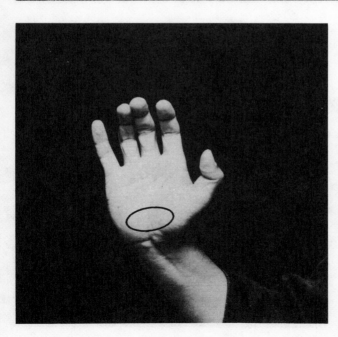

PALM HEEL
(Jang-kal)

To form the palm heel, bend your extended fingers and lock your wrist outward. Apply the palm heel for striking and blocking the face, nose, jaw, chin, ribs, and solar plexus.

BALL OF FOOT
(Ap Bal-badak)

To form the ball of foot, stretch your instep as far away from your shin as possible, then lock your toes upward. Apply the ball of the foot when kicking and stamping the jaw, armpits, ribs, knees solar plexus, face, groin, abdomen, and kidneys.

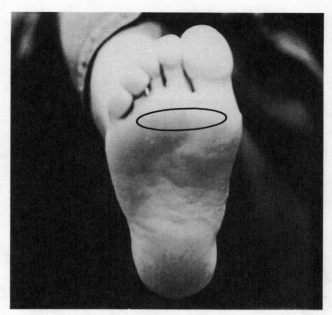

FOOT EDGE
(Bal-nal)

To form the foot edge, extend the outward edge of your foot downward, then lock your toes upward. Apply the foot edge when kicking and stamping the jaw, armpits, ribs, knees, and solar plexus.

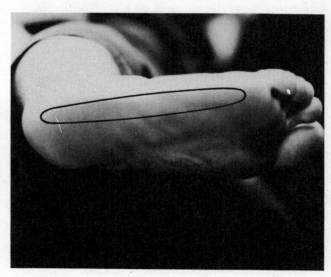

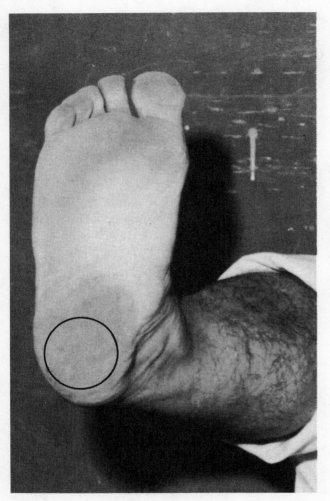

HEEL
(Dui Kum Chi)

To form the heel, stretch your instep as close to your shin as possible with your heel extended outward. Apply the heel when kicking and stamping the jaw, temple, ribs, kidney, groin, and solar plexus.

WARM-UP EXERCISES

Since the body should be in peak condition when responding to arduous training, performing warm-up exercises is considered a vital component in the practice of tae kwon do. Warm-up exercises loosen the muscles and joints, and bring the body to a proper level of performance. These exercises should be performed with the mind relaxed, while concentrating on the approaching practice session. In this way, the mind and body are placed under control to work as a unit while training.

The exercises should also be performed after the practice session in order to, once again, loosen the muscles and joints, and relax the body and mind. No matter how long or short the practice session may be, one should always loosen up, both before and afterwards.

BODY TWISTING

Stand with your feet shoulder-width apart, hands opened or closed at your side. (1) Turn your body to the extreme left, twisting the upper torso further and swinging the arms. (The right foot may be raised at the heel to accommodate the movement.) (2) After completing the turn to the left, twist your body back to the right in the same manner. Do not execute any of these exercises violently; avoid undue strain.

CROSS ARM SQUAT

(1) Stand with your heels together. Cross your arms in front at the belt level. (2) Standing on your toes, raise your arms out to the side. (3) Keeping your body straight, bend at the knees, squat low and cross your arms in front of your body. (4) Rise again to full height, stand on your toes and place your arms out to the side. To finish, assume the original position. The exercise should be performed in a relaxed manner, moving smoothly and rhythmically. One full movement takes a four count. Execute a minimum of five times.

CHEST SPREADING

Stand with your feet shoulder-width apart, hands at your side. Step 45 degrees to the left front. Raise your arms straight ahead, then over your head. Stretch your chest out and forward. Assume your original position and execute the exercise to your right side, following the patterns as given. Practice a minimum of four times to each side.

SIDE BENDING

Stand with your feet slightly more than shoulder-width apart with your left hand at your waist. Raise your right arm to shoulder level, so it is bent upward from the elbow. Lean your body to the left from the waist, bending as far as you can without undue strain. Return to your original position and repeat. Reverse your hand positions and execute twice to your right side. Execute this exercise a minimum of four or five times to each side.

FORWARD BENDING

Stand with your feet almost twice your shoulder-width apart, and your hands on your hips. (1) Bend forward and down from your waist, touching the floor with your fingertips or palms. (2) Bend your body backwards, hands on hips, placing your head far back. Repeat the entire exercise at least five or six times.

LEG STRETCHING

Stand with your legs slightly more than twice your shoulder-width apart, and your hands on your hips. (1) Bend your right leg, lower your body to the right and extend your left leg straight outward with your left foot pointing up. (2) Move slowly and smoothly without undue strain and lower your leg all the way down. Then reverse your position and execute the exercise to your left side, stretching your right leg. If you cannot stretch all the way to the floor, then complete the exercise only as far as you can. Repeat three to five times with each leg.

KNEE BENDING

Stand with your feet together and your hands at your sides. (1) Raise up on your toes, lifting your hands straight out in front of you at shoulder level. (2) Bend from the knees, lower your body, and drop your hands

toward the floor. (3) Rise to full height on your toes and swing your arms straight up over your head. Your arms should swing freely in a relaxed manner. Assume your original stance. Repeat the exercise five to seven times.

1

2

3

NECK TWIST

(1) Stand with your feet shoulder-width apart and let your head fall backwards. (2) Let your head fall forward. (3) Rotate the head clockwise twice. (4) Rotate the head counter-clockwise twice. Repeat the exercise slowly at least twice.

4

DEEP BREATHING

(1) Place your feet shoulder-width apart and cross your hands in front of your body. (2) Move your hands out to the side, keeping your arms straight. Inhale deeply through the nose. Return to your original position, exhaling and relaxing the body. Repeat the exercise four to six times.

1

2

STANCES

Stances play a significant role in many types of physical conditioning. In tae kwon do, a stance provides correct balance, stability, and a strong base from which techniques can be executed. Training in the proper stances augments mind and body coordination, which in turn enhances posture, balance, technique execution, and body shifting.

FRONT VIEW

ATTENTION STANCE
(Cha-ryot So-ki)

Stand with your fists clenched at your side. Place your feet, heels touching, at a 45 degree angle.

FRONT VIEW

NATURAL OPEN FOOT STANCE
(Pal-ja So-ki)

Stand with your fists clenched at your side. Place your feet, a shoulder-width apart, at a 45 degree angle facing outward.

NATURAL CLOSED FOOT STANCE (An-jong So-ki)

Stand with your fists clenched at your side. Place your feet, a shoulder-width apart, at a 45 degree angle facing inward.

FRONT VIEW

CROSSED FOOT STANCE (Go-ah So-ki)

Stand with your fists clenched at your side. Cross your right foot over your left foot, placing the right toes at a 45 degree angle.

FRONT VIEW

FRONT VIEW

HALF SITTING STANCE (OPEN KNEE) (Ju-chum So-ki)

Stand with your feet a shoulder-width apart. Tuck your fists (palms up) at your waist. Bend your knees slightly, facing outward.

SIDE VIEW

HALF SITTING STANCE (CLOSED KNEE) (Murup So-ki)

Stand with your feet a shoulder-width apart. Tuck your fists (palms up) at your waist. Bend your knees slightly, facing inward.

FRONT VIEW

FRONT VIEW

FORWARD STANCE (Ap Guppiki)

Step forward with your left foot. Bend the front knee so the calf is perpendicular to the floor. Lock your back knee in place. This stance places 60 percent of the weight on your front leg and 40 percent on the back leg. The side view shows two shoulder-widths between the legs while the front view indicates one shoulder-width between the legs.

SIDE VIEW

BACK STANCE
(Dui Guppiki)

Move your right leg backward and to the side at a 90 degree angle. Keep your front leg pointed straight ahead. The two legs should be shoulder-width apart, with 70 percent of the weight on your right leg and 30 percent on your front leg.

FRONT VIEW

SIDE VIEW

FRONT VIEW

CRANE STANCE
(Ue-bal So-ki)

Place your hands on your hips. Stand on one leg, bending slightly. Place the other foot behind the knee of the balancing leg.

BACK VIEW

CAT STANCE
(Goyang-yi So-ki)

Place one foot backward at a 45 degree angle. Keep the other foot near you and pointing straight ahead with the heel raised. This stance balances 90 percent of the weight on the back foot and 10 percent on the front foot.

FRONT VIEW

SIDE VIEW

BLOCKS

Good blocking is the key to good defense. Thus, blocking practice is one of the most important phases of tae kwon do training. The majority of blocking is performed with the hands and arms by hooking, deflecting, and striking, in order to halt the opponent's attack. To produce maximum effect, the power in the blocks can be focused on the opponent's attacking leg or arm, which would then discourage further attack. In the event that a counterattack or a second block is necessary, balance and posture should be maintained.

51

1

RISING BLOCK
(Olryo Mak-ki)

(1) Assume a forward stance. Clench your fists and cross your arms in front of your chest. (2) Raise your blocking arm to five inches from your forehead. Angle your arm slightly downward and block with your outside forearm. Pull your second fist to your waist in a ready position.

2

APPLICATION

1

DOWN BLOCK
(Ha-che Mak-ki)

(1) Assume a forward stance. Clench both fists. Raise your blocking fist to your opposite shoulder while pointing the second fist toward the opposite knee area. (2) Pull your blocking hand down, stopping about six inches above the knee. Block with your outside forearm and outside hammer fist. Pull your second fist to your waist in a ready position.

2

APPLICATION

KNIFE HAND
CENTER BLOCK
(Jang-kal Jung-che Mak-ki)

(1) Assume a forward stance. Keep both hands in a knife hand position. Raise your blocking hand across to your opposite shoulder. Place your second hand downward and behind you. (2) Pull your blocking hand in front of your chest as you rotate your arm to block with the outer edge of the knife hand. Place your second hand in front of your solar plexus.

INSIDE CENTER BLOCK
WITH BACK STANCE
(Ahn Jung-che Mak-ki)
with (Dui Guppiki)

Assume the back stance. Clench your fists. Raise your blocking fist to the side at shoulder height. Place the second fist at your waist in a ready position. Pull your blocking fist across in front of your chest, blocking with your outside forearm.

APPLICATION

OUTSIDE CENTER BLOCK WITH BACK STANCE
(Bakat Jung-che Mak-ki) with (Dui Guppiki)

(1) Assume the back stance. Clench both fists. Bring your blocking fist across to your opposite waist. Place your second fist forward and out. (2) Pull your blocking fist out in

APPLICATION

SIDE VIEW

front of your chest as you rotate your arm to block with the inside of your forearm. Pull your second fist to your waist in a ready position.

SIDE VIEW

MOUNTAIN BLOCK
(San Mak-ki)

Assume a stance with your feet placed at a distance twice the length of your shoulders. Face your opponent sideways and clench your fists. With your arms at shoulder level, raise both of your fists high. Twist your upper torso so that you face your opponent. Then return to your original position and, using your outside forearm, block your opponent's technique with an inward strike.

APPLICATION

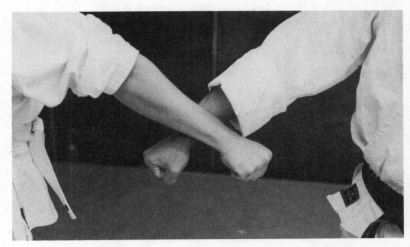

This close-up denotes a variation of the Mountain Block. With your hands stretched outward and downward, block your opponent's technique with the inside of your forearm.

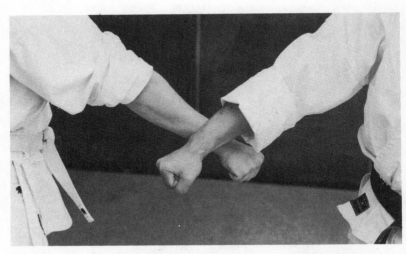

This close-up denotes a variation of the Mountain Block. With your hands stretched outward and downward, block your opponent's technique with the outside of your forearm.

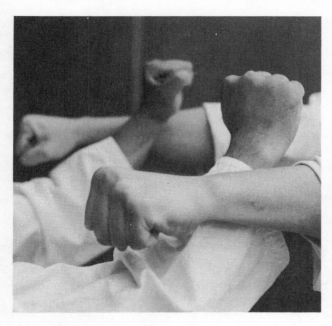

WEDGE BLOCK
(Hecho Mak-ki)

Clench your fists. Cross your arms in front of your chest. Block simultaneously with your outside forearms.

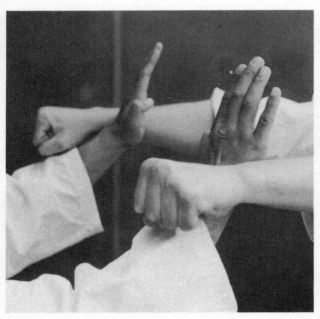

DOUBLE KNIFE HAND BLOCK
(Sang Jang Kal Mak-ki)

Form the knife hand with both of your hands. Cross your arms in front of your chest. Block simultaneously with your outside forearms.

DOWNWARD
PUSHING BLOCK
(Nul-lo Mak-ki)

With an open hand, push your opponent's hand (or foot) downward.

PUSHING BLOCK
(Miro Mak-ki)

With an open hand, use your palm to push your opponent's hand (or foot) to the side.

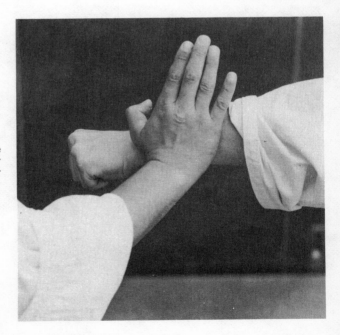

STRIKES

The following techniques are the most common strikes used in the Palgue Il Jang, Yi Jang and Sam Jang Hyungs.

INSIDE NECK STRIKE (Ahn-uro Chi-ki)

(1) Assume a forward stance. Raise your striking hand slightly behind your head in a knife hand position. Extend your other hand forward in a clenched fist position. (2) With your knife hand, strike out and forward in an arc parallel to the floor at neck level. Turn your hand inward, striking with the outer knife edge of your hand. Place your second hand, with the fist clenched, in a ready position at your waist.

MIDDLE LUNGE PUNCH
(Ban-dae Jiru-ki)

(1) Assume a forward stance, with your punching fist clenched and palm up in a ready position at your waist. Extend your other hand forward in a clenched fist position with your palm down. (2) Take a straight step forward with your rear leg, assuming a forward stance. Punch straight forward with your fist, rotating the fist palm downward and parallel to the floor at shoulder level. Place your other hand, with the fist clenched and palm up, in a ready position at your waist.

PALGUE HYUNGS
(FORMS)

According to ancient oriental philosophy, Palgue means "providence of the universe." Palgue represents the father, the mother, the sons and the daughters, as well as the four points of the compass, and the four seas which bound the earth. The Korea Tae Kwon Do Association created eight Palgue hyungs (forms) for use by white belt through brown belt students. The first three hyungs of the Palgue forms are illustrated in this book.

The Palgue hyungs are divided into the following:

GRADE	HYUNG (FORM)
Eighth Grade and under	Palgue Hyung Il Jang (No. 1)
Seventh Grade	Palgue Hyung Yi Jang (No. 2)
Sixth Grade	Palgue Hyung Sam Jang (No. 3)
Fifth Grade	Palgue Hyung Sa Jang (No. 4)
Fourth Grade	Palgue Hyung O Jang (No. 5)
Third Grade	Palgue Hyung Yuk Jang (No. 6)
Second Grade	Palgue Hyung Chil Jang (No. 7)
First Grade	Palgue Hyung Pal Jang (No. 8)

There are nine hyungs required for advancement through black belt from 1st to 6th dan. They are as follows:

DAN	HYUNG (FORM)
First Dan	Koryo Hyung
Second Dan	Kum 'Kang Hyung
Third Dan	Tae 'Baek Hyung
Fourth Dan	Baek 'Jae Hyung
	Ship 'Jin Hyung
Fifth Dan	Jee 'Tae Hyung
	Chun 'Kwon Hyung
Sixth Dan	Han 'Soo Hyung
	Shilla Hyung

PALGUE IL JANG 1

Palgue Il Jang Hyung, designed for white belt students, primarily consists of twenty basic defensive hand movements.

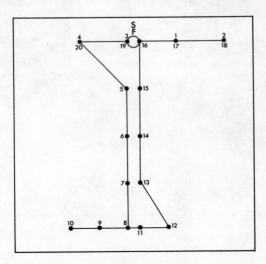

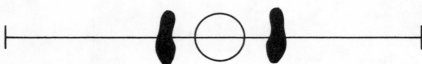

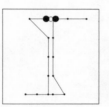

Assume a ready stance with your feet shoulder width apart and parallel. Your fists should be clenched at the abdomen, your body held erect, and your eyes directed forward.

NOTE: All pivotal turns indicated in degrees, either clockwise or counterclockwise, refer to the directional turn of the face. Star symbols (★) indicate KEEHOP (yelling).

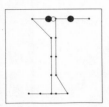

From the starting position, circle your left foot 90 degrees counterclockwise toward position 1 while pivoting on your right foot, assuming a left forward stance as you execute a low block with your left forearm.

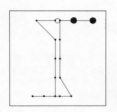

Take a straight step forward with your right foot toward position 2, assuming a right forward stance as you execute an outside middle block with your right forearm.

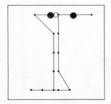

Circle your right foot 180 degrees clockwise toward position 3 while pivoting on your left foot, assuming a right forward stance as you execute a low block with your right forearm.

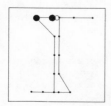

Take a straight step forward with your left foot toward position 4, assuming a left forward stance as you execute an outside middle block with your left forearm.

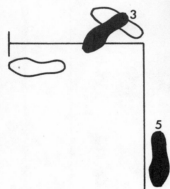

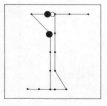

Circle your left foot 90 degrees counterclockwise toward position 5 while pivoting on your right foot, assuming a left forward stance as you execute a low block with your left forearm.

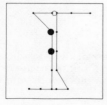

Take a straight step forward with your right foot toward position 6, assuming a left back stance as you execute an outside middle block with your right forearm.

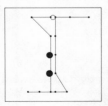

Take a straight step forward with your left foot toward position 7, assuming a right back stance as you execute an outside middle block with your left forearm.

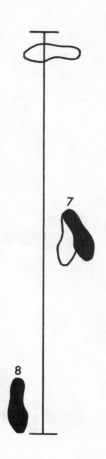

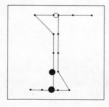

Take a straight step forward with your right foot toward position 8, assuming a right forward stance as you execute a middle lunge punch with your right fist. ★

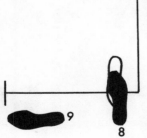

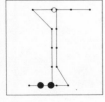

Circle your left foot 270 degrees counterclockwise toward position 9 while pivoting on your right foot, assuming a right back stance as you execute a knife hand center block with your left knife hand.

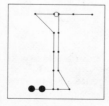

Take a straight step forward with your right foot toward position 10, assuming a left back stance as you execute an outside middle block with your right forearm.

11 9

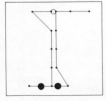

Circle your right foot 180 degrees clockwise toward position 11 while pivoting on your left foot, assuming a left back stance as you execute a knife hand center block with your right knife hand.

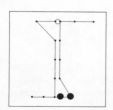

Take a straight step forward with your left foot toward position 12, assuming a right back stance as you execute an outside middle block with your left forearm.

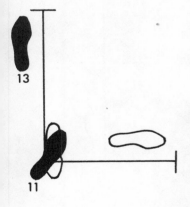

13

11

SIDE VIEW

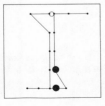

Circle your left foot 90 degrees counterclockwise toward position 13 while pivoting on your right foot, assuming a left forward stance as you execute a low block with your left forearm.

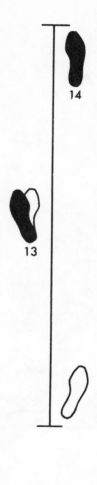

14

13

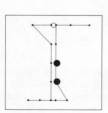

SIDE VIEW

Take a straight step forward with your right foot toward position 14, assuming a right forward stance as you execute an inside knife hand strike to the neck with your right hand.

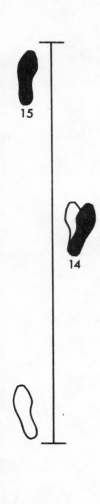

SIDE VIEW

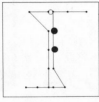

Take a straight step forward with your left foot toward position 15, assuming a left forward stance as you execute an inside knife hand strike to the neck with your left hand.

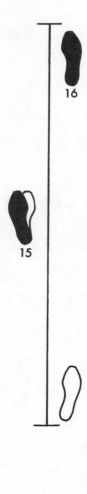

16

15

SIDE VIEW

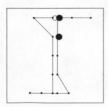

Take a straight step forward with your right foot toward position 16, assuming a right forward stance as you execute a middle lunge punch with your right fist. ★

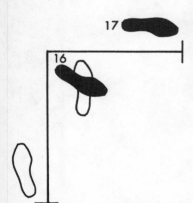

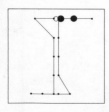

Circle your left foot 270 degrees counterclockwise toward position 17 while pivoting on your right foot, assuming a left forward stance as you execute a low block with your left forearm.

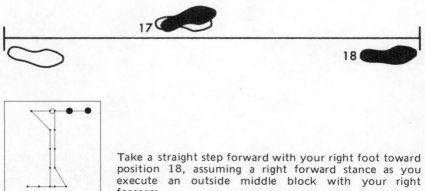

Take a straight step forward with your right foot toward position 18, assuming a right forward stance as you execute an outside middle block with your right forearm.

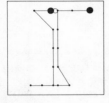

Circle your right foot 180 degrees clockwise toward position 19 while pivoting on your left foot, assuming a right forward stance as you execute a low block with your right forearm.

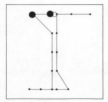

Take a straight step forward with your left foot toward position 20, assuming a left forward stance as you execute an outside middle block with your left forearm.

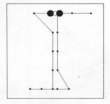

Circle your left foot 90 degrees counterclockwise toward the finishing position while pivoting on your right foot, assuming a ready stance, your feet shoulder width apart and parallel, your fists clenched at the abdomen, and your body erect.

PALGUE YI JANG 2

Palgue Yi Jang Hyung, designed for yellow belt students, primarily consists of twenty offensive-defensive combinations which enhance training in hand and foot coordination.

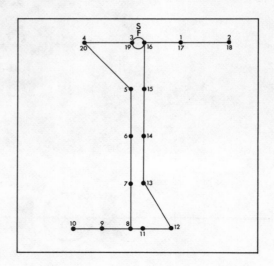

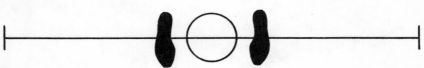

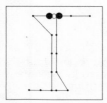

Assume a ready stance with your feet shoulder width apart and parallel. Your fists should be clenched at the abdomen, your body held erect, and your eyes directed forward.

NOTE: All pivotal turns indicated in degrees, either clockwise or counterclockwise, refer to the directional turn of the face. Star symbols (★) indicate KEEHOP (yelling).

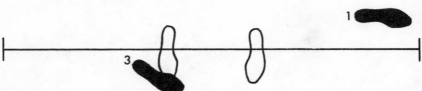

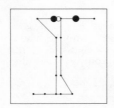

From the starting position, circle your left foot 90 degrees counterclockwise toward position 1, assuming a left forward stance as you execute a rising block with your left forearm.

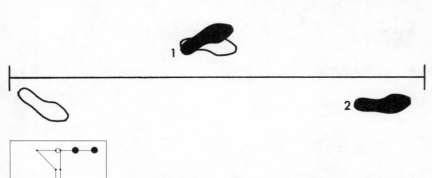

With your right foot, execute a middle front snap kick toward position 2 without changing your hand positions. After recoiling the kick, place your right foot toward position 2, assuming a right forward stance as you execute a middle lunge punch with your right fist.

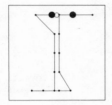

Circle your right foot 180 degrees clockwise toward position 3 while pivoting on your left foot, assuming a right forward stance as you execute a rising block with your right forearm.

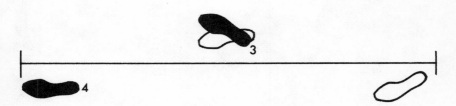

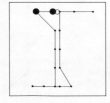

With your left foot, execute a middle front snap kick toward position 4 without changing your hand positions. After recoiling the kick, place your left foot toward position 4, assuming a left forward stance as you execute a middle lunge punch with your left fist.

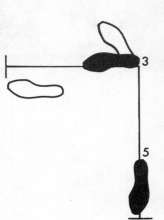

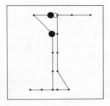

Circle your left foot 90 degrees counterclockwise toward
position 5 while pivoting on your right foot, assuming a
right back stance as you execute a low knife hand block
with your left hand while placing your right knife hand
in front of your solar plexus.

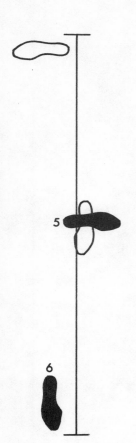

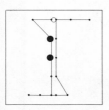

Take a straight step forward with your right foot toward position 6, assuming a left back stance as you execute a knife hand center block with your right knife hand.

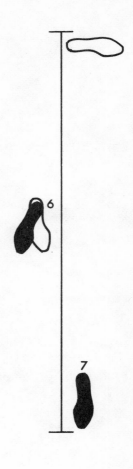

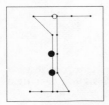

Take a straight step forward with your left foot toward position 7, assuming a left forward stance as you execute a rising block with your left forearm.

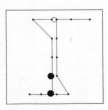

Take a straight step forward with your right foot toward position 8, assuming a right forward stance as you execute a middle lunge punch with your right fist. ★

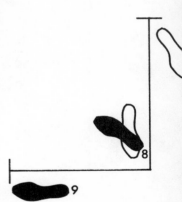

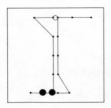

Circle your left foot 270 degrees counterclockwise toward position 9 while pivoting on your right foot, assuming a left forward stance as you execute a rising block with your left forearm.

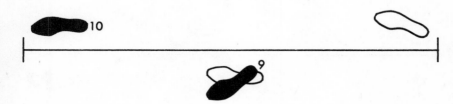

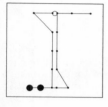

With your right foot, execute a middle front snap kick toward position 10 without changing your hand positions. After recoiling the kick, place your right foot toward position 10, assuming a right forward stance as you execute a middle lunge punch with your right fist.

9

11

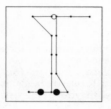

Circle your right foot 180 degrees clockwise toward position 11 while pivoting on your left foot, assuming a right forward stance as you execute a rising block with your right forearm.

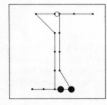

With your left foot, execute a middle front snap kick toward position 12 without changing your hand positions. After recoiling the kick, place your left foot toward position 12, assuming a left forward stance as you execute a middle lunge punch with your left fist.

SIDE VIEW

13

11

Circle your left foot 90 degrees counterclockwise toward position 13 while pivoting on your right foot, assuming a right back stance as you execute a low closed fist block with your left hand while placing your right closed fist in front of your solar plexus.

SIDE VIEW

Take a straight step forward with your right foot toward position 14, assuming a left back stance as you execute an outside middle closed fist block with your right hand while placing your left closed fist in front of your solar plexus.

SIDE VIEW

Take a straight step forward with your left foot toward position 15, assuming a right back stance as you execute an inside middle block with your left forearm.

SIDE VIEW

Take a straight step forward with your right foot toward position 16, assuming a right forward stance as you execute a middle lunge punch with your right fist. ★

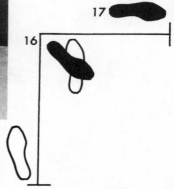

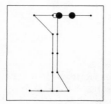

Circle your left foot 270 degrees counterclockwise toward position 17 while pivoting on your right foot, assuming a left forward stance as you execute a rising block with your left forearm.

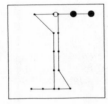

With your right foot, execute a middle front snap kick toward position 18 without changing your hand positions. After recoiling the kick, place your right foot toward position 18, assuming a right forward stance as you execute a middle lunge punch with your right fist.

19

17

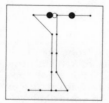

Circle your right foot 180 degrees clockwise toward position 19 while pivoting on your left foot, assuming a right forward stance as you execute a rising block with your right forearm.

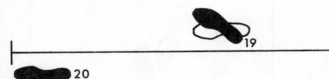

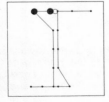

With your left foot, execute a middle front snap kick toward position 20 without changing your hand positions. After recoiling the kick, place your left foot toward position 20, assuming a left forward stance as you execute a middle lunge punch with your left fist.

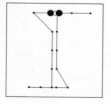

Circle your left foot 90 degrees counterclockwise toward the finishing position while pivoting on your right foot, assuming a ready stance, your feet shoulder width apart and parallel, your fists clenched at the abdomen, and your body erect.

PALGUE SAM JANG 3

Palgue Sam Jang Hyung, also designed for yellow belt students, primarily consists of twenty offensive-defensive movements which enhance training in fast-slow execution of combinations.

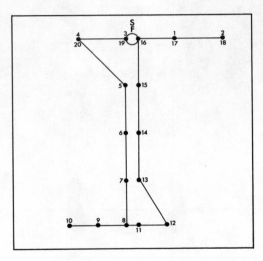

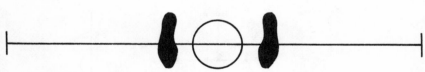

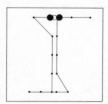

Assume a ready stance with your feet shoulder-width apart and parallel. Your fists should be clenched at the abdomen, your body held erect, and your eyes directed forward.

NOTE: All pivotal turns indicated in degrees, either clockwise or counterclockwise, refer to the directional turn of the face. Star symbols (★) indicate KEEHOP (yelling).

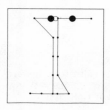

From the starting position, circle your left foot 90 degrees counterclockwise toward position 1 while pivoting on your right foot, assuming a left forward stance as you execute a low block with your left forearm.

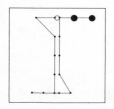

Take a straight step forward with your right foot toward position 2, assuming a right forward stance as you execute a middle lunge punch with your right fist.

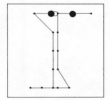

Circle your right foot 180 degrees clockwise toward position 3 while pivoting on your left foot, assuming a right forward stance as you execute a low block with your right forearm.

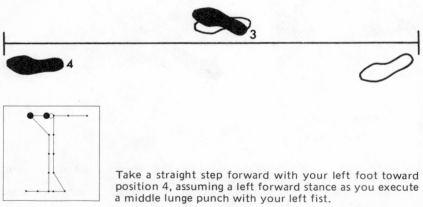

Take a straight step forward with your left foot toward position 4, assuming a left forward stance as you execute a middle lunge punch with your left fist.

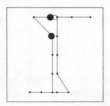

Circle your left foot 90 degrees counterclockwise toward position 5 while pivoting on your right foot, assuming a left forward stance as you execute a low block with your left forearm.

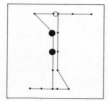

Take a straight step forward with your right foot toward position 6, assuming a right forward stance as you execute a rising block with your right forearm.

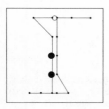

Take a straight step forward with your left foot toward position 7, assuming a left forward stance as you execute a rising block with your left forearm.

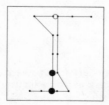

Take a straight step forward with your right foot toward position 8, assuming a right forward stance as you execute an upper lunge punch with your right fist. ★

Circle your left foot 270 degrees counterclockwise toward position 9 while pivoting on your right foot, assuming a right back stance as you execute a knife hand center block with your left knife hand.

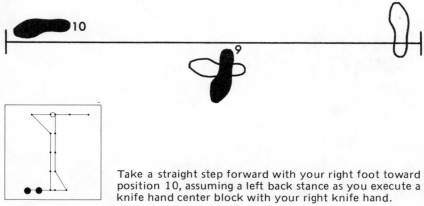

Take a straight step forward with your right foot toward position 10, assuming a left back stance as you execute a knife hand center block with your right knife hand.

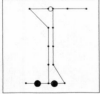

Circle your right foot 180 degrees clockwise toward position 11 while pivoting on your left foot, assuming a left back stance as you execute a knife hand center block with your right knife hand.

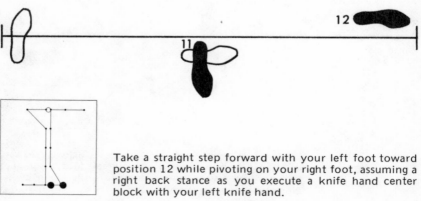

Take a straight step forward with your left foot toward position 12 while pivoting on your right foot, assuming a right back stance as you execute a knife hand center block with your left knife hand.

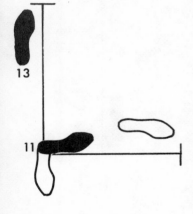

SIDE VIEW

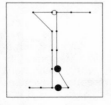

Circle your left foot 90 degrees counterclockwise toward position 13 while pivoting on your right foot, assuming a right back stance as you execute an outside middle block with your left forearm.

13

11

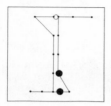

Turn your body in place 180 degrees clockwise while pivoting on both feet, assuming a left back stance as you execute an outside middle block with your right forearm. (This movement and the preceding movement are done in fast combination.)

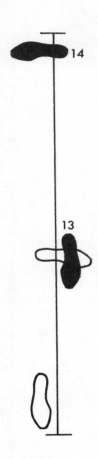

14

13

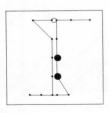

Take a straight step backward with your right foot toward position 14 while pivoting on your left foot, assuming a right back stance as you execute an outside middle block with your left forearm.

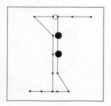

Take a straight step backward with your left foot toward position 15 while pivoting on your right foot, assuming a left back stance as you execute an outside middle block with your right forearm.

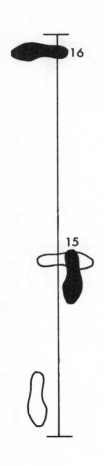

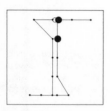

Take a straight step backward with your right foot toward position 16 while pivoting on your left foot, assuming a right back stance as you execute an outside middle block with your left forearm.

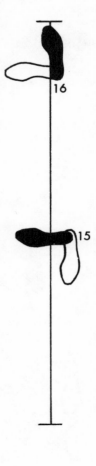

16

15

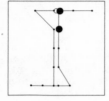

SIDE VIEW

Turn your body in place 180 degrees clockwise while pivoting on both feet, assuming a left back stance as you execute an outside middle block with your right forearm. (This movement and the preceding movement are done in fast combination.)

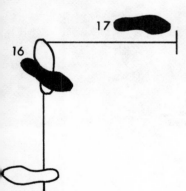

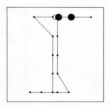

Circle your left foot 270 degrees counterclockwise toward position 17 while pivoting on your right foot, assuming a left forward stance as you execute a rising block with your left forearm.

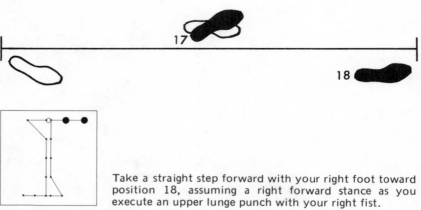

Take a straight step forward with your right foot toward position 18, assuming a right forward stance as you execute an upper lunge punch with your right fist.

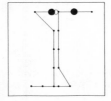

Circle your right foot 180 degrees clockwise toward position 19 while pivoting on your left foot, assuming a right forward stance as you execute a rising block with your right forearm.

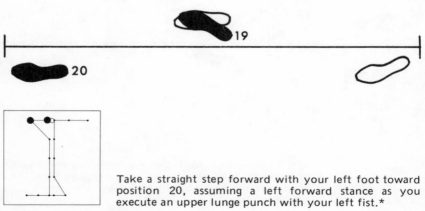

Take a straight step forward with your left foot toward position 20, assuming a left forward stance as you execute an upper lunge punch with your left fist.*

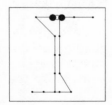

Circle your left foot 90 degrees counterclockwise toward the finishing position while pivoting on your right foot, assuming a ready stance, your feet shoulder-width apart and parallel, your fists clenched at the abdomen, and your body erect.

MATCH RULES
OF TAE KWON DO

Established on November 3, 1962 by the Korea Tae Kwon Do Association and amended four times, the rules contain 14 articles. The following is a summary of the competition rules, as amended on March 7, 1967:

1. Officials shall include one chief umpire, four deputy umpires and two juries. The juries may not be changed during the meet.

2. The umpires, certified as 4th dan black belt or over by the Association, must have passed the examination qualifying a referee. They must have no record of punitive measures by the Association or any other sports organization. The chief umpire is chosen from among the senior members and must have a higher grade of dan than the deputy umpires. The jury is selected from among the men of the 6th dan or over.

3. The chief umpire is the referee and declares the beginning and the ending of the competition. The deputy umpires record both winning and losing points on the scoring paper. The jury must immediately render judgement of any error made by the umpires.

4. Points are scored as follows:
   attack by fist . . . 1 point
   attack by foot
       (a) at the opponent's face . . . 2 points
       (b) at the other parts of the body . . . 1 point
   When the following parts of the body are successfully attacked, points will be scored:
       (a) solar plexus
       (b) both sides of the chest
       (c) both shoulders
       (d) face (attacks by foot only)
5. The matches consist of two ninety-second rounds with a thirty-second recess between rounds.
6. The following violent actions lose points:
       (a) tackling, wrestling or attacking a downed opponent
       (b) attacking the private parts of the body or butting
       (c) attack with fist or elbow to the opponent's face
       (d) intentionally wasting time
       (e) any verbal or physical expression of protest
           against an official's decision

TARGET AREAS

During competition, attacks to the following parts of the body are not permitted.

FRONT OF THE BODY

Skull
Bridge of the Nose
Temple
Sternum
Armpit
Inner Wrist
Groin
Knee Joint
Shin
Instep

BACK OF THE BODY

Base of the Skull
Back of the Neck
Upper Back
Center of the Back
Kidney
Lower Back
Coccyx
Back of the Knee
Achilles Tendon

Attacks by
Fist or Foot
to Solar Plexus

**Attacks by
Fist or Foot
to Side of Chest**

Knife Hand
Attack to Neck

**Attacks by
Foot to Face**

PROTECTION GEAR
FOR SPARRING COMPETITION

Safeguards are protective garments worn by tae kwon do competitors to protect themselves from serious injury. Their use is mandatory in all sanctioned contests or exhibitions. Vital parts of the body protected by these special garments or protection gear are the torso and the groin.

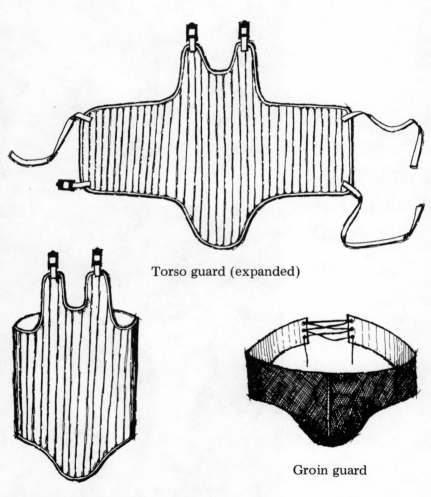

Torso guard (expanded)

Torso guard (as worn)

Groin guard

TAE KWON DO TERMS

ANKLE	BAL-MOK SO-KI
AT EASE STANCE	PYUNI
ATTENTION	CHA-RYOT
ATTENTION STANCE	CHA-RYOT SO-KI
ATTENTION STANCE (BOTH FEET TOGETHER)	MO-AH SO-KI
BACK FIST	DUNG JU-MOK
BACK KICK	DUI CHA-KI
BACK STANCE	DUI GUPPIKI
BALL OF FOOT	AP BAL-BADAK
BEGIN	SHEE-JAK
BENT WRIST	KOM-BE-SON
BODY SHIFTING	OM-KYO DIDI-KI
BOTTOM FIST (DOWNWARD)	ME-JU-MOK
BOTTOM FIST (SIDEWAY)	YOP JU-MOK
BOTTOM HEEL	DUI-CHUK
BOW	KYONG-YE
BREAKING	KYOK-PA
CAT STANCE	GOYANG-YI SO-KI
CENTER BLOCK (MIDSECTION)	JUNG-CHE MAK-KI
CENTER PUNCH	JUNG-CHE JIRU-KI
CHESTNUT FIST (MIDDLE FINGER ONE-KNUCKLE FIST)	BAM JU-MOK
COMPETITION	KYONG JENG or SHEE-HAP
CRANE STANCE	UE-BAL SO-KI
CRESCENT KICK	BAN-DAL CHA-KI
CROSSED FOOT STANCE	GO-AH SO-KI
DIRECTOR, SIR	KWAN-JANG-NIM
DOUBLE JUMP KICK	MODUM-BAL CHA-KI
DOUBLE KNIFE HAND BLOCK	SANG JANG-KAL MAK-KI
DOWN BLOCK (LOW SECTION)	HA-CHE MAK-KI
DOWNWARD BLOCK	NERYO MAK-KI
DOWNWARD PRESSING BLOCK	NUL-LO MAK-KI
DOWNWARD STRIKE	NERYO CHI-KI
ELBOW	PAL-KUP
FIST	JU-MOK
FOOT	BAL
FORM	HYUNG or PUM-SE
FORWARD STANCE	AP GUPPIKI
FRONT BLOCK	AP MAK-KI
FRONT JUMP KICK	DU-BAL DANG-SANG
FRONT KICK	AP CHA-KI
HALF SITTING STANCE (OPEN KNEE)	JU-CHUM SO-KI
HALF SITTING STANCE (CLOSED KNEE)	MURUP SO-KI
HIGH FRONT FLYING KICK	DUI-MYO NOPPI HA CHA-KI
HORSE RIDING STANCE	MURUP SO-KI
INDEX FINGER FIST	INJI-JU-MOK
INNER WRIST	AHN PAL-MOK
INSIDE BLOCK	AHN MAK-KI
INSIDE STRIKE	AHN-URO CHI-KI
INSTEP	BAL-DUNG
INSTRUCTOR, SIR	SABOM-NIM
JUMP ROUNDHOUSE KICK	DUI-MYO DOL-RYO CHA-KI
JUMPING KICK	DUI-MYO CHA-KI
KICKING	CHA-KI

KNEE KICK . . . . .MURUP CHA-KI
KNIFE HAND . . . . JANG-KAL or SON-NAL
KNIFE HAND (SIDE) . . . . .YOP JANG-KAL
KNIFE HAND CENTER BLOCK . . . . JANG-KAL JUNG-CHE MAK-KI
LEG STRETCH . . . . .CHA OL-RI-KI
LOW PUNCH . . . . HA-CHE JIRU-KI
MARTIAL ART SCHOOL . . . . DO JANG
MOUNTAIN BLOCK . . . . SAN MAK-KI
NATURAL STANCE (OPEN FOOT) . . . . PAL-JA SO-KI
NATURAL STANCE (CLOSED) . . . . .AN-JONG SO-KI
ON GUARD . . . . .GO-MAHN
ONE FINGER SPEAR HAND . . . . HAN-SON-KUT or HAN-SON KWAN-SU
ONE STEP . . . . HAN-GORUM
ONE STEP SPARRING (PREARRANGED) . . . .HAN-BON MATCHU-O KYORU-KI
OPEN KNUCKLE FIST . . . . PYUN JU-MOK
OUTSIDE BLOCK .BAKAT MAK-KI
OUTSIDE CENTER BLOCK . . . . BAKAT JUNG-CHE MAK-KI
OUTSIDE STRIKE . . . . BAKAT CHI-KI
OUTSIDE WRIST . . . . .BAKAT PAL-MOK
PALM HEEL . . . . .JANG-KAL or BATANG
PEACOCK HAND . . . . .SON-KUT CHO-KI
PREARRANGED ATTACK . . . . .MATCHU-O KYORU-KI
PLIERS HAND . . . . JIP-GAE-SON
PROTECTIVE ARMOR . . . . .HO-GOO
PUPIL . . . . SURYUN-SENG
PUSHING BLOCK . . . . .MIRO MAK-KI
RAKE HAND . . . . .GAL-QUI-SON
READY . . . . .JUN-BEE
READY STANCE . . . . JUN-BEE SO-KI
RELAX . . . . SHEE-YO
REVERSE PUNCH . . . . BARO JIRU-KI
RIDGE HAND . . . . OPPUN JANG-KAL
RISING BLOCK . . . . OLRYO MAK-KI
RISING BLOCK (UPPER BODY) . . . . .SANG-CHE MAK-KI
ROUNDHOUSE KICK . . . . DOL-RYO CHA-KI
SELF-DEFENSE TECHNIQUE . . . . .HO-SIN-SUL
SIDE BLOCK . . . . YOL MAK-KI
SIDE JUMP KICK . . . . DUI-MYO YOP CHA-KI
SIDE KICK . . . . .YOP CHA-KI
SPARRING . . . . MAT KYORU-KI
SPEAR HAND . . . . SON-KUT or KWAN-SU
STRAIGHT PUNCH . . . . BAN-DAE JIRU-KI
THREE STEP . . . . .SEGORUM
THREE STEP SPARRING . . . . SEBON MATCHU-O KYORU-KI
TIGER MOUTH HAND . . . . AH-KUM-SON or KAL-JE-BI
TURNING . . . . DOL-KI
TWO FINGER SPEAR HAND . . . . DU-SON-KUT or DU-SON KWAN-SU
UNIFORM . . . . .DO-BOK
UPPER CUT PUNCH . . . . .JECHO JIRU-KI
VERTICAL PUNCH . . . . SEWO JIRU-KI
WEDGE BLOCK . . . . .HECHO MAK-KI
WRIST . . . . PAL-MOK